Contents

Introduction   4

1. The History of Stirling   8

2. The Battles for Stirling   24

3. The Reformation   43

4. Oliver Cromwell in Stirling   62

5. The Jacobite Uprising   76

6. Stirling in More Recent Times   82

Bibliography   95

About the Author   96

Introduction

The military heritage of Stirling, one of Scotland's smallest yet most fought-over cities, can be traced back for centuries. It is Stirling's position, at the lowest crossing point of the River Forth, that makes it such an important location for both invaders from the south and the occupants in the north.

Although it is known that the area has been occupied for over 4,000 years, the earliest recorded inhabitants were the Celtic Maeate tribe, who dominated the region with many strongholds in the hills surrounding modern-day Stirling. During the first-century Roman invasion of the lands now known as Scotland, the River Forth was a major obstacle for the advancing legions. Yet despite attempts to secure the crossing at Stirling, it is believed General Agricola, the Roman governor of Britain, ended up using the riskier option of the islands in the Firth of Forth as a crossing point, indicating they had been unable to defeat the Maeate. While the Romans had – and continued to construct – a series of forts around the Stirling area, control was difficult to maintain. Some of these forts formed the Antonine Wall, which runs around 17 miles south of Stirling and was constructed to defend the Roman-held territory from the invaders from the north.

By the seventh century the Romans had long departed and this region of Scotland was occupied by the Picts; however, the lands faced fresh invasions from the expanding Northumbrian kingdom. It is believed a fortification stood on Castle Hill at Stirling by this time, and that it, along with control of the crossing, were successfully taken by the invaders and used to launch a number of triumphant attacks northwards against the Pictish tribes, before they were ultimately forced back and Stirling became under the control of the Pictish tribes once more.

The tenth century saw the tribes of Scotland united to become the first Scots and, although the exact date of the construction of the first royal castle at Castle Hill is unclear, it is known that one stood during the eleventh century, with the town of Stirling starting to grow in the form of wooden huts on the hillside around the castle. The strategic importance of Stirling resulted in the castle being one of the most besieged in Scotland, with it changing hands between the English and the Scottish several times, and extensive damage being caused by both the Scots and the English. Among the battles fought, two of the most

View over Stirling, including the crossing point. (Courtesy of Kim Traynor, CC BY-SA 2.0)

View of Stirling showing the elevated position of the castle in the distance. (Courtesy of Mike Pennington, CC BY-SA 2.0)

With Stirling Castle being sited on a cliff edge, it is clear to see why this position was chosen to build defensive structures for centuries. (Courtesy Kim Traynor, CC BY-SA 2.0)

famous and most decisive clashes in Scottish history – the Battle of Stirling Bridge and the Battle of Bannockburn – were fought at Stirling in the thirteenth and fourteenth centuries.

During the Reformation Stirling faced considerable damage from the internal wars of the divisions within the Christian church, and during the seventeenth century the Lord Protector of the Commonwealth of England, Scotland and Ireland, Oliver Cromwell, set his sights on control of the city to allow the crossing to be utilised for his advance north.

The Act of the Union eventually brought relative peace to Stirling, only interrupted by the Jacobite uprising of 1745 when Bonnie Prince Charlie stayed in the area and sought to gain control of the castle. Stirling did, however, go on to retain its military importance and became home to several regiments of the British army.

Throughout this book I hope to take the reader through some of the key points in history, as summarised above, which had the greatest effect on the town of Stirling and the surrounding area in more detail, explaining the reasons behind the conflicts and impact on not just the region, but on a national scale. I will also explore some of the monuments dedicated to Stirling's military heritage and some of the buildings that still play an important role in this. My intention is to hopefully demonstrate to the reader why it was frequently said, 'He who holds Stirling, holds Scotland.'

1. The History of Stirling

When approaching Stirling from any direction, two poignant reminders of the city's military past can be seen from miles around. The most visible is the National Wallace Monument, perched on top of the hill known as Abbey Craig; the second is Stirling Castle, which sits atop Castle Rock. Throughout this chapter I aim to explore the background of these landmarks and the key stages of Stirling's history, before looking at some of the specific parts in more detail in later chapters.

There can be little doubt that it was the importance of the crossing point at the River Forth that both gave birth to the settlement that would become Stirling, yet also brought so much conflict to the area. The discovery in 1879 of a burial cairn in the Coneypark area of the town revealed just how long the area had been occupied, with the bones found within being carbon dated to be from between 2152 and 2021 BC, making Torbex Tam, as the skeletal remains became known, to be over 4,000 years old. Tam's skull was found to have considerable impact damage to the right side, and with this being the likely cause of death, it is perhaps also an indicator of how long there has been conflict in the area.

As mentioned in the introduction, the earliest occupants of the lands were the Maeatae tribe, who were believed to have had strongholds on Gowan Hill in the town and also on the hill named Dumyat. It is from the name of this hill, derived from the Gaelic 'Dun Maeatae', meaning 'Fort of the Maeatea', that the name of the tribe is known.

The arrival of the Romans between the years 70 and 80 AD brought the first recorded conflict to the area. Marching around the River Forth would result in a significant and dangerous detour inland due to the many associated risks of attack and the inevitable additional time it would take. And so the Roman legions, led by General Gnaeus Julius Agricola, sought the lowest crossing point for the river, which was at Stirling. As they marched north, forts were built along the way, giving nearby defensive positions to not only retreat to if required, but also a supply route for rations and weapons to be brought to consistently keep up with the advancing forces. A number of these forts – Castlecary, Rough Castle and Camelon – are all situated around the Stirling area. It is believed that it was from Camelon that General Agricola launched an attack to try to take the crossing at the Forth. Exactly what happened is not documented, yet with it being said he later made his way across the Forth via the islands, it is fair to assume the attack was unsuccessful.

Stirling, taken from Abbey Craig. (Courtesy of Sonse, CC BY 2.0)

The burial cairn discovered at Coneypark.

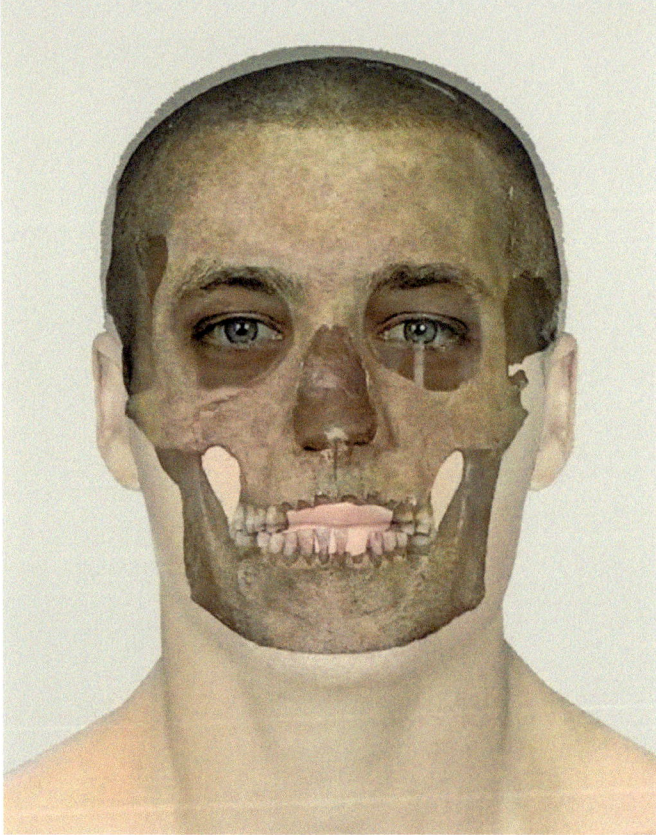

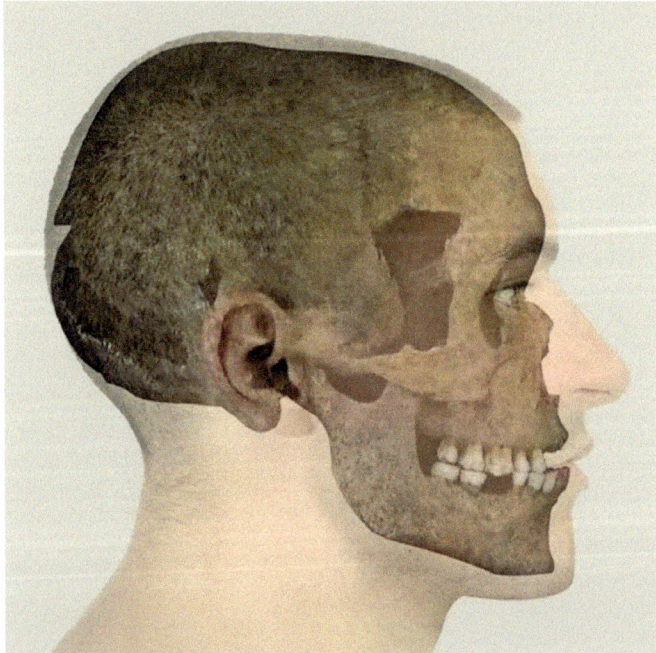

Left and opposite page: The facial reconstruction of Torbrex Tam. (Courtesy of Emily McCulloch)

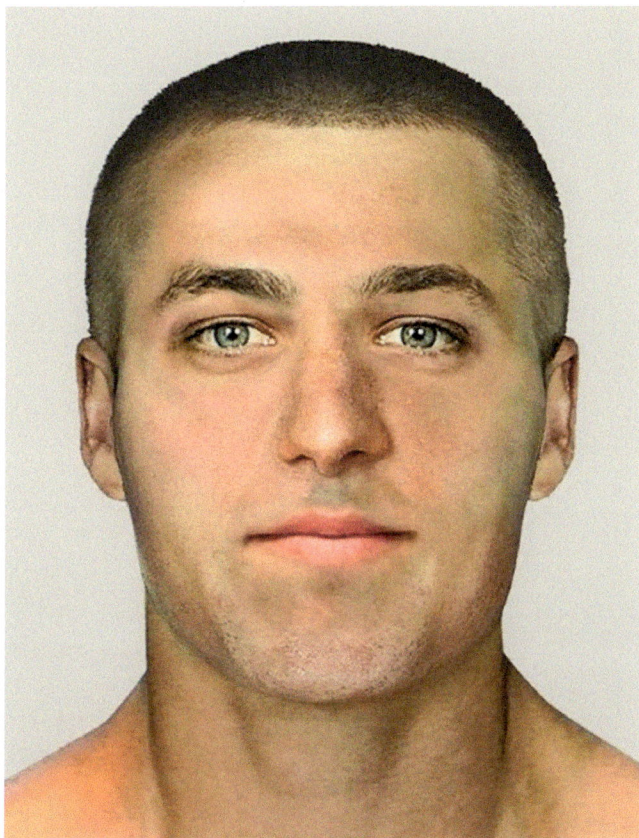

After their success at the Battle of Mons Graupius at a much disputed location in the north of Scotland, the Romans returned, this time leaving their mark on Stirling by building a road between the hills to the north of the site of the current castle and a fort on Motte Hill – on the site of the former Maeatae stronghold. As the Roman forces retreated the local tribes were swift in reclaiming the land to the north of the Forth, resulting in further withdrawal south and Emperor Publius Aelius Hadrianus having his famous wall built to protect the Roman frontier.

His successor, Emperor Antoninus Pius, appointed Quintus Lollius Urbicus as governor of Great Britain, with orders to do as General Agricola had, and to advance north. It is recorded that Lollius put many of Agricola's forts back into use and occupied Stirling, having a residence close to the current castle. Although now sadly lost to weather erosion, historical records tell that an inscription carved into the rocks opposite the castle gates stated that the Roman 11th Legion was stationed there to keep watch. Emperor Antoninus eventually ordered the wall bearing his name be built between the Firths of the River Clyde and the River Forth, marking the new northern frontier of Roman occupied Britain, once again returning Stirling to the control of the local tribes.

The tip of Mote Hill where the Maeatae tribe are believed to have held a hill fort.

View towards Rough Castle Fort. (Courtesy of Lairich Rig, CC BY-SA 2.0)

A section of the base of the Antonine Wall at New Kilpatrick Cemetery. (Courtesy of Lairich Rig, CC BY-SA 2.0)

Successive Roman emperors made further attempts to advance north, with control of Stirling changing hands several times. By the third century a new threat to the Romans was first documented. Known as the Picts, meaning 'the Painted People' due to the warpaint they covered themselves with, they became the dominant force in the east of Scotland. Little is known of their history, largely due to them not having written records. The main direct information from the Picts has to be interpreted from cave carvings they left, with the remainder being taken from the Roman historians, which is likely to be biased against them. The Picts were not content to occupy the territory north of the Antonine Wall and, instead, took the battle to the Romans, launching a number of invasions into Roman Britain, resulting in counter-attacks from the Romans. Probably one of the most decisive battles took place just a few miles from Stirling on the banks of the River Carron at the start of the fifth century. Although the Picts were defeated

Above, below and opposite page: Pictish carvings at the Wemyss Caves in Fife.

by the Romans, both sides suffered heavy losses, with some accounts describing the river running red with the blood of the dead for several miles, and it was just a few years later that the Romans withdrew completely.

Evidence of these early military conflicts remained right up to relatively recent times, with the remains of the Roman fort at Gowan Hill, described as having mounds covering the walls that were tall enough to have hidden a horse and cart, being recorded as late as the eighteenth century. In 2002, while digging trenches to lay cables for floodlighting at the National Wallace Monument on Abbey Craig, the remains of a structure were discovered. Archaeologists assessed that this was a significant fortification, possibly a citadel, dating back to between the sixth and eighth centuries. With it being known that the monarchy of that time would move around their territory, it is believed that this may be the earliest royal household to have existed in Stirling, and a clear sign of the importance the area had.

When the Romans withdrew, the Northumbrians moved into the territory to the south east of modern-day Scotland, expanding their kingdom as far as Stirling, which they occupied to launch attacks further north against the Picts. During the ninth century a new enemy had arrived, with the Picts also facing attacks from the north from the Vikings. This stretched the Pictish forces; yet, it would also lead to the retreat of the Northumbrians, due to the Viking invasions of the land around Berwick effectively cutting off southern Scotland from the rest of the Northumbrian kingdom.

Scotland at that time remained the territory of two opposing nations: the Picts in the east and the Scots in the west. Seeing the Picts facing threats from all sides, the Scots seized an opportunity to attack their weakened long-term foes and take control of all of Scotland. A series of battles were fought between the Scots, with King Kenneth MacAplin of the Scots ultimately claiming the Pictish crown. This position was strongly opposed by Drust X of the Picts, and he claimed the crown for himself. With King Drust holding the stronghold of Stirling, King Kenneth marched towards the town to try to take the town, and crown, by force; however, Drust launched a counter-attack before his forces even made it over the river. The forces of King Kenneth were the victors. With both sides weakened due to their losses peace talks were offered, which soon revealed themselves to be a trap to lure King Drust from the security of Stirling and he, along with any others with potential claims to the Pictish crown, were slaughtered, allowing King Kenneth to unite the kingdoms and form the country known as Alba. The details of the battle north of Stirling, which marked the beginning of the end of the Picts and the creation of the Scottish nation, are somewhat scant. It is, however, believed to have been fought where the sports fields of Stirling University now lie. The battlefield is marked by two large stones in the grounds of the university complex: the 2.7-metre-high Airthrey Stone in the sports fields, and the 2.8-metre-high

The old standing stone near Airthrey Castle. (© Frank Garvock, CC BY-SA 2.0)

Stirling Castle.

The stone bridge that now stands on the site of the original Stirling Bridge. (Courtesy of G. Laird, CC BY-SA 2.0)

Pathfoot Stone. The area became known as Cambuskenneth, meaning 'the Field of the Kenneth', which is believed to refer to the area being a battlefield.

The decision to construct the royal castle at Stirling is a further sign of how important the town was considered. Yet, as was often the case, such a structure brought conflict with it, as opposing forces sought to gain control. William I, better known as Willian the Lion, waged war against King Henry of England over control of Northumberland, and ended up a prisoner of the English as a result. In return for his freedom he signed over control of large parts of Scotland, including Stirling and its castle, to King Henry only for it to be bought back from King Richard, Henry's successor, to aid the funding of the Third Crusade. This was the first of many times control of the castle changed hands, and is notable for being the only occasion when both exchanges were carried out peacefully and without bringing destruction to the town.

The start of the Wars of Independence between England and Scotland would see Stirling a key target, with two of the most famous battles in Scottish history taking place in the town. William Wallace had grown to prominence through his opposition to the English invaders, yet it was the Battle of Stirling Bridge that would make him top of the English ruler's 'most wanted' list. In the early

St Andrews Castle, the Palace of the Archbishop of St Andrews, who was so influential in many of the decisions made by the monarchy in Stirling.

A surviving section of the old town wall. (Courtesy of Robert Murray, CC BY-SA 2.0)

Part of the old town wall below the old jail. (Courtesy of Andrew Smith, CC BY-SA 2.0)

Bastion beside Dumbarton Rock – part of the old town wall. (Courtesy of Lairich Rig, CC BY-SA 2.0)

fourteenth century Stirling was once again under siege when the forces of Robert the Bruce met the forces of Edward II in the fields beside the Bannock Burn.

In 1543, the Treaty of Greenwich was signed, agreeing to the marriage of Mary, Queen of Scots, to Edward, the son of Henry VIII. Both were still infants and so the marriage would not take place for some years, allowing time for suspicion and concern on the motives to be raised and doubt put in the minds of the officials. Despite the treaty including an agreement that guaranteed the independence of both Scotland and England, the union between the monarchy of the two countries would bring its own problems. England had already converted to become a Protestant country, whereas Scotland remained Catholic, although the ripples of the Reformation had already started to be felt. Scotland had also always had strong ties with France, a Catholic country, and supporters of this alliance, including the head of the Scottish Church, Cardinal Beaton, argued that this was an attempt by the Protestant English king to seize control of Scotland. For her own safety, Mary was taken to Stirling Castle, where her coronation was later held to ensure the independence of Scotland.

Stirling town wall's plaque. (Courtesy of Haydn Blackey, CC BY-SA 2.0)

In December 1543 the agreements made under the Treaty of Greenwich were reversed. As a consequence, in 1544 King Henry launched a series of invasions into Scotland – a period known as the Rough Wooing. He was angered that the earlier agreement for Mary, Queen of Scots, to be betrothed to his son was not being honoured and instead opted to try to 'persuade' the Scottish authorities, by force, that the agreed future marriage should go ahead. Leith was to suffer extensively through this period, with it being particularly targeted by the king's commanders. In 1547, work began to construct a new wall to protect Stirling, sections of which can still be seen today. The Statement of National Importance, issued by Historic Environment Scotland, regarding the town wall states:

> The monument represents a significant element in our understanding of the late medieval burgh of Stirling, its extent and the strategic importance it held, first as a seat of royal government, and latterly as one of Scotland's most important garrison towns. Like many of the town defences built at times of crisis, the wall's random rubble fabric may reflect its rapid construction in 1547, when the town represented an important target for English raiders.

There can be no doubt from the above of both the importance of Stirling at this time and the risks the town faced from King Henry's army.

In 1548, after the Scots defeat at the hands of the English at the Battle of Pinkie, agreement was reached between Scotland and France for Queen Mary to marry Francois, the son of Henri II of France, with the terms of the agreement stating that their children would be the future monarchs of both France and Scotland. On 7 August, Queen Mary set sail for the safety of France, where she grew up with her future husband; however, tragedy befell the couple when Henri died in 1560, aged just eighteen years old. With no children Mary was stripped of her title of Queen of France and returned to Scotland. The Scotland she returned to was, however, very different from the one she had left. The Protestant Reformation had taken hold, with destruction to many towns and cities, including Stirling, from the conflict. Mary sought to regain control, spending time at Stirling and having her son James baptised there into the Catholic faith; however, she was matched in power and opposed by John Knox, 'Father of the Protestant Reformation', resulting in her reign being turbulent.

In 1603, Mary's son, James VI, became James I of England – successfully uniting the crowns without bloodshed. Yet any hopes of this union bringing peace were quickly dashed due to the remaining political and religious differences between the two countries. Oliver Cromwell rose to prominence and, as the Lord Commander of the Commonwealth, he waged war against Scotland due to the defiance of the Scottish authorities. Stirling again played a pivotal role as a defensive stronghold and a key crossing for the River Forth. Having been forced back several times, Cromwell took decisive action to cut off Stirling using a high-risk strategy that had never been seen before.

Stirling eventually entered a period of peace, although devastation struck several times in the form of the plague. The town also escaped unscathed during the Jacobite uprisings of 1715 and 1745, despite a short occupation by the forces of Bonnie Prince Charlie. The nineteenth century started to see recognition of Stirling's military prominence, with the construction of the National Wallace Monument. With several regiments of the British army based there, Stirling also became an important recruitment centre during the First World War. Today there are reminders of the military heritage of the area all around the city, and Stirling hosts an annual Armed Forces Day, a military show featuring a parade, military bands and military displays.

2. The Battles for Stirling

With Stirling being situated at such an important and strategic location, it is perhaps not a surprise that it has been the site of some of the most significant battles in Scottish history. The main battles for the town took place during the first Wars of Independence with England, which took place between 1296 and 1328.

The build up to the war started with the death of Alexander III in 1286, when he was tragically thrown from his horse during a storm near Kinghorn in Fife. With no heir to claim the throne, various contenders came forward. One came from the Norwegian authorities who argued that King Alexander's eight-year-old grandaughter, Margaret of Norway, was his closest direct descendant, and so the rightful heir. In an attempt to resolve the matter, the assistance of Edward I of England was sought, and he ruled that it was indeed Margaret who had the strongest claim to the throne. Arrangements were made for her to be brought by boat to Scotland to take her place in the monarchy, but with the caveat that once she was of age she was to be married to King Edward's son, bringing the crowns of Scotland and England to one ruler. Unfortunately, the journey to Scotland was too much for young Margaret, as she died on 26 September 1290, having never reached the shores of Scotland.

Once again, the crown was fought over, with it eventually coming down to two main contenders: Robert Bruce (grandfather to the more famous King Robert the Bruce) and John Balliol. With no end in sight and the matter needing to be resolved once and for all to bring stability back to the country, once again the authorities sought the help of King Edward. Having already lost out on an opportunity to unify the crowns, King Edward did not want to miss his second opportunity. In order to have his decision respected, he asked that both men first accepted him as their overlord, a request that both declined as it would mean, no matter who won the contest, they would be subservient to the English king. They both instead used this to their advantage, pointing out that to recognise King Edward as their overlord would mean handing control of Scotland to him, which was something that could only be done by a king. As neither were yet king, they therefore could not do so, yet would give him their answer once he had appointed one of them into the role.

King Edward's advisors then sought to use the legal system in order to achieve the king's aims. They pointed out that as long as the contest was between two

A memorial marking the approximate spot Alexander III fell to his death near Kinghorn, Fife.

claimants, the king's role was to adjudicate; however, if there were more than two claimants he could simply rule which one was to become heir. With a potential thirteen claimants, both Bruce and Balliol realised that the control of the country was potentially slipping from their grasp, and someone with a weaker claim to the throne could be appointed king over them. As such, both agreed with Edward's demands and accepted him as their overlord, based on his assurances that he would not interfere with the ruling of Scotland.

Having heard both of the cases, King Edward judged that John Balliol had the strongest claim to the throne and he was crowned king. Almost immediately, King Edward began to meddle in Scottish affairs, culminating in a request for Scottish military assistance in his war against France. This placed King Balliol in a precarious situation. Scotland had always had a strong alliance with France, yet he was now being asked to provide an army to aid in England's war against them. In an act of defiance, Balliol declined Edward's request and, in 1296, instead signed an allegiance with France. In response, King Edward sent forces north to invade Scotland, triggering the start of the Wars of Independence. After a decisive victory for the English at the Battle of Dunbar, the humiliated King Balliol was forced to publicly apologise to King Edward, before being stripped of his royal regalia. Several castles, including Stirling, were surrendered to the English forces,

The site of the 1296 Battle of Dunbar. (Courtesy of Richard Webb, CC BY-SA 2.0)

A replica of the Stone of Destiny in the grounds of Scone Palace. The original is held at Edinburgh Castle. (Courtesy of Michael Garlick, CC BY-SA 2.0)

and King Edward had the records of Scotland, and the 'Stone of Destiny', upon which Scottish kings were historically crowned, taken to England in a firm show that he was in control.

The Earl of Surrey, John de Warenne, was left as the warden of Scotland to rule on behalf of the king. He is said to have found the weather too cold and returned to England, saying it was making him ill. There was already a growing uprising in the north of Scotland and, with King Edward no longer having a direct commander in Scotland, the opportunity was seized and attacks were launched on the English, led primarily by William Wallace and Andrew Murray. They swiftly reclaimed large parts of the country and, with most of the territory north of the River Forth under their control, John de Warenne was ordered back to Scotland to clear up the situation he had created and retake control of the country. In order to do so William Wallace knew he would have to use the crossing at Stirling, so they positioned their forces on the north side, awaiting their arrival.

Warenne led a force of around 9,000 men, and when faced by the army of Wallace and Murray it seems he was determined to crush the opposition once and for all. His army was larger and well trained. He knew that with many of the Scottish nobles already defeated at the earlier Battle of Dunbar, their

The replacement stone bridge crossing the River Forth.

The entrance onto the replacement bridge over the Forth gives an idea of the narrow crossing faced by the English forces. (Courtesy of Euan Nelson, CC BY-SA 2.0)

The approximate view William Wallace would have had of Stirling Bridge, which at that time would have been unobstructed. (Courtesy of Allister Combe, CC BY-SA 2.0)

This view over Stirling shows how the river meanders, restricting the area of land available for the English forces to do battle. (Courtesy of Mike Pennington, CC BY-SA 2.0)

trained men were not among the army they now faced. Confident that when seeing the English forces, the Scots would seek to negotiate a settlement, he waited. After several days, however, there was no such approach and Warenne decided to wait no longer. What he hadn't accounted for was the knowledge of the geography of the land that the Scots had. They had largely positioned their army on Abbey Craig, which gave them unrestricted views of the movement of the English. They also knew there was a floodplain with marshland to the north of the river, with a causeway being the only way through it. The width of the causeway would restrict the ability of the English horsemen to spread out once they had crossed the bridge, forcing them to ride no more than two abreast for the full length of it, with the causeway finishing at the base of Abbey Craig. Effectively the English forces were being brought straight to the Scots Army, with Wallace estimating that, given the restrictions of the land, it would take several hours for the whole English army to cross the river.

After two false starts – the first being stopped because Warenne overslept, and the second being because he believed the Scots were about to surrender, only to receive a note stating they were to do battle instead – Warenne ordered his army to move forward. He had put in a request for cavalry to be sent upriver to help cover the crossing, but this was declined by the king's treasurer who, frustrated at the slow progress, ordered him to get on with it and stop wasting time and money.

As the English started to cross, Wallace watched patiently. It would be a fine line between there being enough of the English army across the river for him to have a significant impact, and there being too many for them to defeat. When just over half of the army had crossed, Wallace signalled the attack. Spearmen charged down the causeway, forcing the English to the sides, while others positioned themselves along the riverbank, cutting off their retreat. With the heavy cavalry of the English army caught in the long narrow causeway they were unable to fight back. They could not retreat as the forces had built up behind all the way back to the bridge, and those who were forced to either side of the causeway found themselves stuck in the swampland. The Scots now not only had the advantage of higher numbers, but the English forces were virtually useless due to their surroundings. With all but a few men who were able to avoid the Scottish spearmen and swim back across the river, Warenne ordered the rest of his army back and had the bridge destroyed to prevent the Scots from pursuing him. Having lost an estimated 100 cavalry and 5,000 infantry, he had no option but to take his remaining army back to Berwick to regather, leaving just one garrison to defend Stirling Castle. The Scottish rebellion, however, was motivated after the victory. It had been shown that even the larger, heavily armoured English armies could be beaten, and control of Stirling Castle was soon retaken by the Scots.

The area where the Battle of Stirling Bridge was fought. Note the position of the castle in the background.

The Battle of Stirling Bridge Stone, set in the ground in the shadow of the auld brig of Stirling to commemorate the battle. (Courtesy of Robert Murray, CC BY-SA 2.0)

Plaque to commemorate the battle of 1297 on a plinth situated near the north entrance of the auld brig of Stirling. (Courtesy of Robert Murray, CC BY-SA 2.0)

Memorial stone to Andrew Murray, who led with William Wallace and died from the wounds inflicted during the battle. Sadly the memorial stones are badly weather-worn.

Following his victory at the Battle of Stirling Bridge, William Wallace was appointed guardian of Scotland, a short-lived role that he held until his defeat at the Battle of Falkirk in 1298, following which he was forced to resign and all but disappeared from the historical records. He returned to launch further attacks against the English in 1304, until he was betrayed by a Scottish knight and handed over to King Edward.

Throughout this six-year period, King Edward's campaign in Scotland had continued. Stirling Castle had been taken in 1298, when it was found abandoned after the defeat of Wallace, only for it to be won back by the Scottish forces the following year. The army, which successfully regained control of the castle, included soldiers led by Robert the Bruce, who had been appointed governor of Scotland after the resignation of William Wallace. Stirling remained the thorn in King Edward's side throughout, and by 1304 he had successfully taken control of all of the major strongholds in Scotland, with the exception of Stirling Castle.

Determined to take the castle, and control of Scotland, King Edward launched a large-scale attack. In addition to a formidable army he took twelve fortified, wheeled battering rams, known as siege engines, to try to break down the

The defensive walls around Stirling Castle made it a formidable stronghold. (Courtesy of David Dixon, CC BY-SA 2.0)

A weighted catapult similar to the one used against Stirling Castle by King Edward. (Courtesy of Robin Drayton, CC BY-SA 2.0)

castle's defences. He laid siege to the castle for three months, literally throwing everything he had at it. So many cannonballs were used that the lead had to be stripped from the church roofs to make more and keep up with the demand. The castle was also bombarded with a highly flammable mix known as Greek fire, yet still the Scots within held their position. The situation was becoming desperate for the king, who was not only becoming more and more frustrated the longer the siege lasted, but he was aware he also risked losing support and facing further rebellions if he lost. In addition, he had been struggling raising the funds to maintain his campaign in Scotland and faced desertions within his army. In one final attempt, he had his chief engineer, Master James of St George, draw up plans and then build a massive counterweighted catapult. Known as the WarWolf, it is reported that the castle garrison offered to surrender having seen it being built, but King Edward refused as he was determined to have a show of power.

On 24 July the castle was eventually surrendered. There are conflicting versions of the events. Some accounts state that the moat became so filled with rubble after months of attack that ladders could be used to breach the castle walls; however, it was most likely that it was the use of the WarWolf, destroying the gatehouse, which is likely to have led to another offer to surrender, with it being accepted on this occasion.

It was found that the castle had in fact been held by only thirty men and, in perhaps a sign of respect for their bravery, King Edward had agreed favourable terms for the surrender, although he subsequently had the men imprisoned. The leader of the Scottish garrison and commander of the castle, Sir William Oliphant, was sent to the Tower of London where he subsequently switched alliance to King Edward. By 1309 he was back at Stirling Castle, serving under Edward II of England.

With many of the Scottish nobles having pledged allegiance to the English king, the country could have fallen completely under English rule had it not been for a campaign of resistance. Robert the Bruce led the resistance, with the remaining supporters of King John Balliol recognising Bruce as the King of Scotland – all be it under threat of losing their estate if they had refused. Momentum built as successive strongholds fell to the Scottish forces, with Stirling again being a primary target. The English forces within the town surrendered to Bruce's army and, fearful that the castle garrison may follow suit, Edward II invaded. Sir Philip Mowbray, a Scottish nobleman loyal to King Edward, was governor of the castle at the time. He had faced the forces of Bruce before and, after a long siege, he negotiated a deal that if the English forces did not arrive by 24 June 1314 he would surrender the castle to the Scots.

King Edward had gathered a massive army, estimated to have comprised of around 2,000 horsemen and 25,000 infantry from across England, Wales and

Ireland, making it the largest English-led force to ever invade Scotland. Despite the size of the army, which dwarfed Bruce's forces of around 6,000–7,000, Sir Philip Mowbray knew that the Scottish forces remained a significant threat, and he met with King Edward on 23 June to urge him not to go into battle. Although smaller in number, King Robert's army was split into three divisions: one led by the king himself and the other two led by his brother Edward and his nephew Thomas. After years of guerrilla warfare, which had successfully taken back most of Scotland, the infantry were skilled soldiers, yet King Edward ignored the warnings.

The deal made with Mowbray gave King Robert a significant advantage. He knew King Edward would be bringing forces from the south and he could focus his attention to them, as a victory would also secure the castle. His knowledge of the local terrain was also advantageous, as he could choose a location to meet the English forces that most suited his own army's battle techniques. The land to the south of Stirling, partially bordered by the Bannock Burn and with several patches of marshland, was picked. The woodland around would provide cover for his men and escape routes if necessary, while all of these factors would present obstacles to King Edward's horsemen. Having refused to pay heed to the warnings given to him, Edward continued north and met King Robert's forces.

After a short initial battle between a division of the English cavalry headed by Sir Henry de Bohun and one of the divisions of the Scottish army, with neither side gaining the upper hand, the Scots moved back into the woodland. Seeing this as a retreat, the cavalry followed; however, Bohun spotted King Robert himself and, sensing an opportunity for an early victory, he guided his horse towards the king. Bruce avoided the initial attack, yet swung his axe as Bohun passed, crushing the Englishman's head. Seeing their commander struck down, the cavalry started to fall into some disarray; however, they regrouped under Sir Henry Beaumont and Sir Robert Clifford, and continued their pursuit of the Scots forces.

Unknown to them, Scottish reinforcements awaited them within the woodland. With no cover from archers, and their movements confined by the trees along with fresh ditches dug in preparation by the Scots, the cavalry struggled to match the Scottish forces, mainly comprising of spearmen, and they retreated to once again regather. With night falling, a battle that King Edward had seemingly thought would be over relatively quickly (few battles of that era lasted more than a few hours) was about to go into its second day. This gave time for the English forces to reflect on what had happened, which brought further unrest to them. Fearing further attacks under the cover of the darkness, they moved to the opposite side of the Bannock Burn to give themselves some protection before setting up camp, although it is said little sleep was had, with the commanders remaining on edge of the Scottish tactics. Plans were drawn up to try and lure King Robert out into an open battlefield where they would be able to put the Welsh bowmen into action, making them confident they would be victorious.

The Scottish forces, however, were in high spirits. They saw the first day of battle as a victory and, encouraged by motivational speeches by King Robert, they were driven and optimistic going into the second day. Sir Alexander Seton, a Scottish knight and captain of Berwick Castle who had sided with King Edward initially, defected overnight. He brought the news of the position of the English camp, and that they remained largely in formation rather than resting due to fear of a further attack. He also told that the English were deflated after their initial defeat and urged King Robert to take the battle to King Edward while his army remained demoralised.

The view of Stirling Castle from Bannockburn.

View of the battlefield at Bannockburn. (Courtesy of Stanley Howe, CC BY-SA 2.0)

The Bannockburn Heritage Centre, operated by the National Trust for Scotland, where all information relating to the battle can be found. (© Stanley Howe, CC BY-SA 2.0)

The Battle of Bannockburn had a wide-reaching effect. This memorial plinth is at Ceres in Fife, dedicated to those from the village who lost their life. (© Stanley Howe, CC BY-SA 2.0)

The Bannock Burn, close to the battlefield. This small burn caused considerable problems to the heavy cavalry of the English army. (Courtesy of Robert Murray, CC BY-SA 2.0)

Statue of the king.

It was, without a doubt, a risky move and seemed to play right into the hands of the English. The following morning King Robert marched his army from the woods towards the English camp. In these deeply religious times the outcome of battles were often seen as the judgement of God and, keen to keep his own side's morale high, Bruce had delivered a speech invoking the power of St Andrew, the patron saint of Scotland, to provide religious protection for his men. He also had the Abbot of Arbroath march with his army, carrying relics of St Columba. As the English watched, the Abbot of Inchaffrey moved to the front and delivered Mass and blessings for the Scottish army. Seeing them kneel, King Edward was sure they were in the process of surrendering and seeking mercy, to which it is said his advisors replied that they were indeed seeking mercy, but not from King Edward. They were making their peace with God, a sure sign that none would flee the fight and it would be a fight to the death.

As the battle started, the Welsh bowmen commenced fire on the Scottish lines. The Scots quickly formed into schiltroms (a large, tight formation using overlapping shields for protection) and advanced. Cavalry attacks were launched by the Earl of Gloucester and Sir Robert Clifford, yet with the schiltroms forming large obstacles, surrounded by spears, they proved almost impenetrable. The English cavalry found themselves being pushed into a restricted space and the Welsh bowmen were ordered to cease fire as they were striking the English forces. The Scots cavalry advanced on the archers, cutting them down.

Meanwhile hand to hand battle took place in the centre of the battlefield, with both sides seemingly evenly matched until Bruce advanced his own schiltrom. With fresh, highly experienced fighters entering the battle, the English forces began to give way and were forced backwards towards the burn. With the Scots clearly gaining the upper hand, King Edward was escorted away from the battlefield by his men, initially seeking shelter in the safety of Stirling Castle. They did, however, find the castle secure, with Sir Mowbray having already decided that if the English army was to fall then the castle was sure to pass to the Scots, either through the agreed surrender or by force, and so it was an unwise place for King Edward to be.

On the battlefield, the English army disintegrated. With King Edward being escorted away, along with his royal standard, panic set in. The retreating army were hemmed in by their own forces behind, who could not move back due to the river and the ditches the Scots had dug. It is estimated that hundreds of both men and horses drowned trying to flee. The English losses were considerable – said to have been around 100 knights and thousands of infantry. King Edward himself was pursued by Sir James 'The Black' Douglas, and only narrowly escaped when he was able to board a waiting ship at Dunbar. The Scots, however, are estimated to have lost only two knights, along with several hundred infantrymen. True to his word, when he learned of the final outcome of the battle Sir Phillip Mowbray relinquished control of Stirling Castle to King Robert the Bruce, and also swore allegiance to the king. Sir Philip went on to fight alongside Edward Bruce, until he was killed in battle in 1318. One of King Robert's first actions after securing Stirling Castle was to order it be destroyed, to prevent it falling into English hands and being used against the Scots again.

The outcome of the Battle of Bannockburn was not just significant for Stirling, but significant for the whole country. Bruce was in control of Scotland, and in return for the release of English nobles that had been taken prisoner he was able to secure the release of Scottish prisoners from King Edward's captivity, including members of his own family. The battle was seen as the beginning of the end of the first War of Independence; however, although King Robert had effectively secured Scottish independence, it was not until the Treaty of Northampton came into force in 1328 that it was officially recognised.

View of Stirling Castle.

Stirling Castle. (Courtesy of Graham Drew, CC BY 2.0)

3. The Reformation

When thinking of the military impact on a country, region or town it is natural for the mind to conjure images of invading forces bringing warfare with them; however, some of the conflicts were internal and, in Scotland, one of the most decisive in shaping the country was the Protestant Reformation.

Before exploring the impact on Stirling, it is important to set out the circumstances around the Reformation to put matters into context. Scotland was a Catholic country, as were most countries across Europe at the time. The Church had a considerable role in the running and decision making of the country, leading from its headquarters at the cathedral and Archbishop's Castle in St Andrews. Such was the level of influence, St Andrews was often referred to as Scotland's Rome. It is even reported that King Robert the Bruce rode his horse down the central aisle of St Andrews Cathedral. In 1517, a movement started in mainland Europe that would sweep from country to country, and change the religious map forever.

St Andrews was not only the home of the Catholic Church in Scotland, it was also the home of one of the top universities, which ultimately brought the Reformation right to the door of the archbishop. A young man named Patrick Hamilton had spent time in Europe before returning to Scotland to take up his studies at St Andrews. While studying at Paris, he had heard the preaching and read the writings of Reformation leaders such as Martin Luther and, perhaps rather naively, he was keen to spread the word among his fellow students in St Andrews of what he had learned. Needless to say, word soon reached Archbishop James Beaton, who sought to quell any potential influence Hamilton may have. Hamilton realised the danger he was in and fled to mainland Europe once again, yet soon returned, his faith being strong enough that he would face whatever was in store for him. After seemingly being allowed to continue with both his studies and preaching unchallenged, Archbishop Beaton invited Hamilton to his castle to meet. Almost immediately, the young student was arrested and charged with heresy. On 29 May 1528 a short show trial took place, where thirteen charges were put to Hamilton and, upon his refusal to deny the writings of Martin Luther, he was sentenced to death by means of being burned at the stake. To minimise any risk of backlash, the sentence was carried out the same day, with the execution site being in front of St Salvator's Chapel, the university's own Catholic church. In the haste there was little time

The ruins of St Andrews Cathedral dominate the town's skyline. The remains of the castle can be seen to the right. (Courtesy of Kyle R. Stewart Photography)

for preparation and the execution was botched. The quantity of wood was both insufficient and too wet to allow the flames to take hold, and Patrick Hamilton suffered at the stake for six hours before he finally perished. While Archbishop Beaton's intention had been to stop the Reformation in its tracks, the suffering of Hamilton had the opposite effect, with the townspeople and fellow students seeing only the barbarity of the Church. Realising there was public unrest, Beaton's advisors recommended that no more reformers should be publicly executed, but Beaton did not listen. In 1533, he had the reformer Henry Forrest burned at the stake on high ground so that the flames would be seen for miles around as a warning.

Support for the Reformation continued, yet it was the actions of Cardinal David Beaton, nephew and successor to Archbishop John Beaton, that would ultimately lead to the end of the rule of the Catholic Church in Scotland. Beaton had lost favour after the death of King James when he produced falsified papers to try to act as regent to the infant Queen Mary, which would have put him in charge of the monarchy and Church. Having failed, he turned his attention back to the reformers who continued to threaten the authority he still held. One preacher named George Wishart particularly caught his attention.

St Salvator's Chapel in St Andrews, outside which Patrick Hamilton was burned to death.

The letters 'PH' in the pavement mark the spot where Hamilton was burned to death.

Wishart had established a considerable following and was travelling from town to town delivering sermons. Beaton initially tried to discredit him and funded an assassination attempt. Then, when all else failed, he lured Wishart into a trap, had him arrested and burned at the stake outside St Andrews Castle. During the execution Cardinal Beaton was observed lounging in his private quarters within the castle, watching Wishart's agony as he burned. While he was congratulated by his fellow Church leaders, he had miscalculated the support George Wishart had. Just a few weeks later ten of Wishart's allies snuck into the castle under the guise of being workmen and seized control, before brutally murdering the cardinal and hanging his body from the very window from which he had watched the execution. They held the castle for almost a year in the knowledge that King Henry of England had already started to attack Scotland under the period known as the 'Rough Wooing', discussed earlier in the book, and they hoped Henry's Protestant forces would arrive to free them. Unfortunately, with the Scottish authorities seeking the aid of France (still a Catholic country) it was their navy who arrived first, and with the castle being bombarded from the ships in the bay, those inside soon surrendered. They did, however, opt to offer their surrender to the French and were taken as galley slaves. Among them was John Knox, a former bodyguard for George Wishart and a man who would later rise to prominence.

Upon his release John Knox returned to England, before marching an army back to Scotland, to Edinburgh and to St Giles Cathedral. Having entered the building unopposed, he delivered a powerful sermon and just a few days later was elected Minister of St Giles, with the Catholic symbology being removed. John Knox's return, and the influence he had, caused great difficulty in Scotland. The country was being ruled by Mary of Guise, acting as regent for her daughter, Mary, Queen of Scots, who was still in France. Both were devout Catholics, and with French troops remaining in Scotland as part of the agreement relating to the safe passage of Queen Mary to France, the relationship between Scotland's administration and the Protestant Church leaders was, at best, strained and confrontational, with

The letters 'GW' set in the road outside St Andrews Castle mark the spot George Wishart was put to death.

The statue of John Knox, in a rather sorry state, in Stirling's Old Town Cemetery.

John Knox originally being declared an outlaw before a reluctant acceptance of his authority as his support grew.

In 1558, following a proclamation made at the Market Cross in Edinburgh forbidding any form of preaching without the authority of the bishops, and instructing the people of Scotland to prepare celebrations for Easter, according to the rites of the Catholic Church, a number of reformers were summoned to Stirling. Paul Methven, John Christison, William Harlaw and John Willock were all known Protestant preachers and the queen regent hoped that by making an example of them in Stirling, the people would fall into line behind her orders and return to the Catholic churches. They were charged with administering the sacrament of the altar without permission and in a manner different from that of the Catholic Church, and by doing so seducing the people who attended to their erroneous doctrines. A trial date was set for 10 May, with a number of town burgesses becoming the guarantors for their appearance.

In private, a number of high-level supporters of the Protestant movement who also had a level of support for the queen regent urged her not to proceed with the trial and reminded her of a number of promises she had previously made. Yet she initially refused to do so, stating that all of their preachers were to be banished from Scotland. On reflection, and under threat of losing their support, she went on to agree not to go ahead, before once again changing her mind. John Knox, having recently returned to Scotland from France, wrote a letter stating that, as she had decided to go ahead with the trial, he too would be present in Stirling to support the preachers. This was a high-risk move: he knew that to voluntarily appear at a predetermined location on a set date may well lead to his arrest and trial for heresy. The threat of the fiery preacher who could command so much support through his use of words acting to defend the preachers had however caused some concern within those leading the prosecution.

Along with a large number of principal reformers from Renfrewshire and Angus, John Knox approached Stirling; yet, in an attempt to avoid confrontation, he sent John Erskine of Dun ahead to meet with the queen regent. A deal was struck that in return for John Knox to cease his advance on Stirling, the queen regent would not go ahead with the trial. However, once again she went against her word and, on the day of the trial, proceeded. The preachers were declared outlaws due to failing to appear and those who had offered security were fined for their non-attendance.

John Erskine delivered the news to the Protestant leaders in Perth, where Knox was, after which a number of unfortunate events led to the destruction of a Catholic Church by supporters of the Reformation. This was seized upon by the queen regent, who summoned all of the country's nobles to Stirling to emphasise the danger they faced from the Reformation, leading to an increase in hostilities on both sides and the country being on the verge of a full-scale civil war.

With relations with the queen regent at breaking point, the Protestant leaders decided to impose their faith as the prominent religion across the country, with it being agreed to commence in St Andrews. Knox had always hoped that he would one day be able to preach at St Andrews once again, and willingly accepted an invite to meet with the prior of the abbey. As he approached the town on 9 June 1559, word reached him that the archbishop had formed an armed guard, with strict instructions to fire upon him if he attempted to preach from the pulpit at the cathedral. Discussions took place and, with uncertainty regarding the feelings of the people of St Andrews towards the Reformation along with the threat to Knox, it was recommended that he should not preach. John Knox, however, was not to be held back. The following day he delivered a sermon – uninterrupted. Over the following days he continued to deliver sermons, firing up the townsfolk with his passion, leading to the provost, baillies and people of the town to agree to establish reformed worship within the town, with the Catholic churches being stripped of their imagery and the start of the destruction of the monasteries, including the great cathedral.

The queen regent was residing in her palace in Falkland, Fife, at the time and, having been kept up to date with the developments at St Andrews, decided to take action. The information passed to her were that the Reformation leaders had a relatively small guard with them, so she sent her troops to the town to confront them. Reformers from Angus, however, had learned of her plans and sent forces to intercept her, with the two armies meeting just outside Cupar. Rather than risk a battle with a larger force, the queen regent agreed to a truce, whereby she would withdraw all French troops from Fife and send commissioners to St Andrews to negotiate a resolution to the opposing side's differences. While

The ruins of St Andrews Cathedral. (Courtesy of Douglas Nelson, CC BY-SA 2.0)

Falkland Palace, where the queen regent made plans to fortify Stirling Bridge. (Courtesy of Sheila Winstone, CC BY-SA 2.0)

the troop withdrawal did happen, no commissioners were sent, which raised suspicion. It was subsequently discovered that the queen regent had withdrawn to Stirling with her French troops, where she was attempting to fortify the crossing of the River Forth in order to cut off communications and supplies between the reformers north and south of the river, thereby weakening their forces. The leaders of the Reformation acted quickly and sent an army to Stirling to take the town before the bridge was secured. The queen regent retreated to Dunbar, leaving Stirling undefended. While decisions made in the town had led to devastating effects elsewhere, the full destructive force of the Reformation had arrived in Stirling.

John Knox undertook a tour of preaching across lowland Scotland, including Stirling, resulting in the Catholic clergy being driven from their buildings, which were subsequently destroyed. In Stirling, the Monastery of the Black Friars, a Dominican friary established in 1233 dedicated to St Laurence, which stood around Murray Place and Maxwell Place in the town, and the Franciscan Priory of the Grey Friars, founded in 1494 by James IV, which stood close to the town wall between Spittal Street and Albert Place, were destroyed.

Cambuskenneth Abbey was another victim of the Reformation. Founded around 1140 by David I to act as an abbey for Stirling Castle. Its connection to the royal household brought it great wealth. A ferry once operated carrying worshipers across the Forth from Stirling to the abbey, which grew to a considerable size through the thirteenth century. Originally occupied by the canons of the French Arrouasoan Order, the abbey was later controlled by Augstinian canons, who were responsible for praying for the monarchs of Scotland. They were also responsible for administration roles, and after his victory at Bannockburn, King Robert the Bruce held parliament there. The abbey is also the final resting place for James III and his queen, Margaret of Denmark. Yet this counted for nothing when it came to the Reformation. The abbey structure was largely destroyed and, rather than be driven from it, or worse, several of the monks converted to the new faith. Several artefacts from the abbey were taken, including the massive bell from the tower; however, the bell was so heavy that the boat carrying it away sunk and it is said to still lie on the bed of the Forth. The stone from the abbey, as with the other monasteries, were used in the construction of several buildings around Stirling and for later works to the castle.

The most visible sign of the Reformation in Stirling is the Church of the Holy Rude. A church has stood on the site, close to Stirling Castle, since the 1130s, with the name 'Holy Rude' meaning Holy Cross. A fire that swept through Stirling in 1405 destroyed most of the town, including the church, and it was after this that work on the building that stands there today started. The first stage of the new church was the part that now forms the nave and the lower portion of the tower, which allowed worship to once again take place on the site by the end of the fifteenth century. Phase two of its development saw the construction of the east end of the church, during which time the tower was also heightened. A third stage was planned, which would add a large central tower as well as heighten the nave to match the choir and balance the church, but the Reformation caused the work to be stopped before it was completed, leaving the church with its unusual appearance that remains today.

Towards the end of 1559, the town council of Stirling sought to cease the destruction of its religious establishments and voted to renounce their support for Catholicism and move Stirling forward under the Protestant faith. While this may have ended much of the destruction around Stirling, the effects of incidents and decisions made in the town continued to affect the country as a whole. When the queen regent died a new treaty was agreed, known as the Treaty of Leith, which saw the withdrawal of the remaining French troops in Scotland and closer ties with neighbouring England. In 1560, the Scottish Parliament abolished the papal authority in the country, recognising the Protestant faith instead. The following year, in 1561, Mary, Queen of Scots returned to Scotland after the death of her husband in France – a Catholic queen in a Protestant country. With

A footbridge now sits where a ferry used to transport worshippers to the abbey from Stirling. (© Richard Webb, CC BY-SA 2.0)

The ruins of Cambuskenneth Abbey.

The Church of the Holy Rude, which was left with uncompleted work due to the Reformation.

John Knox at the head of the Protestant Church they formed an uneasy truce, yet sought to overthrow each other. Mary married her cousin, Lord Darnley, and in June 1566 she gave birth to their son, James. To the dismay of the authorities of the country, Mary had James baptised into the Catholic faith at Stirling Castle, an action that sent shock waves across Scotland's hierarchy as to the queen's intentions. The following year, Lord Darnley died in mysterious circumstances, following which she soon married her third husband, James Hepburn, Earl of Bothwell. This marriage was deeply unpopular, with suspicion falling not only on Hepburn for being responsible for the death of Lord Darnley, but on Mary herself, leading to the Protestant leaders having her arrested and imprisoned at Loch Leven Castle. Prince James was kept safe at Stirling Castle, where Mary was allowed to visit him on several occasions before she finally abdicated and he was anointed King of Scots at the Church of the Holyrude in Stirling. During his coronation John Knox delivered a sermon in which he called for Queen Mary to be executed, although it seems even the authorities deemed this an inappropriate action at the coronation of her son, and decided against his calls.

Loch Leven Castle, where Mary, Queen of Scots was imprisoned from 1567 to 1568.

These events once again brought military intervention to Stirling. In the period between Queen Mary's arrest and the crowning of King James, his grandfather, Matthew Stuart, the 4th Earl of Lennox, was appointed as regent. Queen Elizabeth of England, however, opposed this and waged war against him. While he was holding parliament in Stirling on 3 September 1571, an army sent by Queen Elizabeth stormed the town and seized Lennox and a number of his supporters, who they took as prisoners. The Earl of Mar, however, brought aid from the castle, who, together with the townsfolk, successfully fought back against the queen's forces. In the battle, one of the leaders of the invaders, Claud Hamilton, the Earl of Huntly, ordered that the Earl of Lennox be shot rather than risk him be freed. He was replaced as regent by the Earl of Mar for a period of one year, during which

The Martyr's Monument in Stirling's Old Town Cemetery, which depicts the sad image of an angel watching over two young girls, Margaret and Agnes Wilson, who were arrested for holding the Protestant faith. Margaret was put to death by being tied to a stake below low tide and drowned.

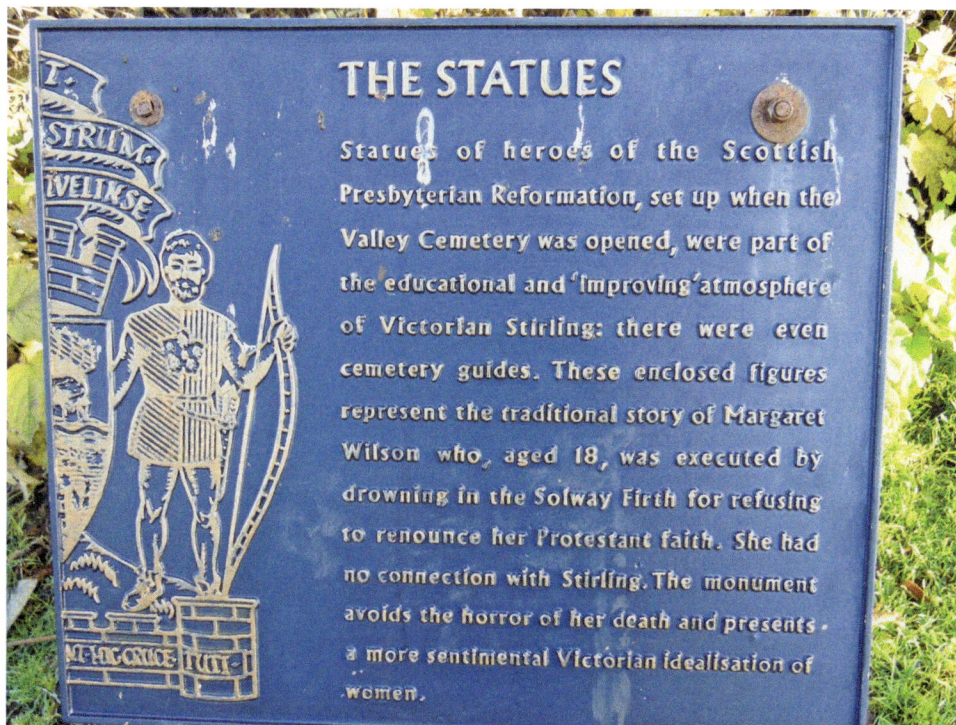

The memorial plaque for the Martyr's Monument.

Ebenezer Erskine statue, Old Town Cemetery. (Courtesy of Kim Traynor, CC BY-SA 2.0)

Andrew Melville statue, Old Town Cemetery. (Courtesy of Kim Traynor, CC BY-SA 2.0)

Alexander Henderson statue, Old Town Cemetery. (Courtesy of Kim Traynor, CC BY-SA 2.0)

James Renwick statue, Old Town Cemetery. (Courtesy of Kim Traynor, CC BY-SA 2.0)

time, as a great moderator, he managed to restore relative peace to Scotland. A number of monuments stand in the town's Old Cemetery to commemorate these times and those who played a later role in the Reformation in Scotland.

Some of the secrets of this period in Stirling's history were uncovered as recently as 2014 when work was being carried out close to the railway station and the remains of a building were uncovered. Archaeologists were brought in and they discovered that the building was in fact the remains of the Black Friars monastery. A large-scale excavation was carried out, revealing the previously unknown true extent of the building. A human skeleton was also discovered, which, due to the burial position and artefacts found with the body, it was possible to identify as being the remains of one of the canons. Further analysis confirmed the bones to be that of a man, aged between twenty and thirty-five years old, and from a time period between 1271 and 1320.

4. Oliver Cromwell in Stirling

Without a doubt, one of the most famous and infamous, figures in British history is Oliver Cromwell. His invasion of Scotland with his New Model Army was a turbulent time, and one when control of Scotland was all but taken by an English invader, and it was during this invasion that his desire to secure Stirling was such that he risked it all in an ambitious and unorthodox manner to seize control of the town.

Before exploring the effects on Stirling, it is important to initially give some background context into Cromwell's ambitions. In 1603, when Queen Elizabeth I of England died with no direct heirs, the English crown was passed to her closest living relative, that being her cousin, King James VI of Scotland. The union of the crowns of Scotland and England, a desire that had been fought over for centuries, was achieved with no bloodshed. Yet this was not a time for most to rejoice. While the monarchs had long desired bringing the crowns together, the nobles, parliaments and churches had not. Both countries had very different needs and functioned to attend to these needs. Even the reformed churches had differing beliefs. The English parliament made things very difficult for the Scottish King, protecting their own authority to the detriment of the monarchy. When King James passed in 1625, he had achieved few of the significant changes he had hoped to, and so his son, Charles I, hoped to achieve what his father had not when he succeeded him to the throne. Unfortunately, Charles too soon discovered just how difficult a task that would be, with religion and the authority of the church leaders remaining a major obstacle.

A new religious movement, known as the Covenanters, had risen in Scotland with ambitions to retain the Scottish Presbyterian doctrine, and they had the support and abilities to go to war to achieve it. King Charles willingly took the battle to the Covenanters, yet his campaigns were unsuccessful. With the English Parliament seeing the Covenanter movement as an internal Scottish issue and not their concern, they started to lose patience with the king's actions and his wasteful use of money and resources. With the relationship between the king and Parliament breaking down completely and England entering into civil war, a back-up plan had been put in place to ensure that the country could be defended. The New Model Army was the result, so called for the simple reason it followed a new model as opposed to the previous methods to put together an army, creating full-time, professional soldiers who could be called upon to do battle anywhere in the country. To support the Parliamentarian cause, a deal was struck with the Scottish Covenanters in an agreement known as the Solemn League and Covenant, in which the support of the Covenanter army was pledged in return for the Scottish Presbyterian doctrine being protected and expanded. This brought the Scottish Parliament, who still supported King Charles and the Royalist cause, into conflict with the Covenanters.

In 1647, the Scottish Covenanter forces handed King Charles over to the English Parliament, and in 1648 the consequences of the English Civil War, which had expanded to Scotland and Ireland and become known as the War of the Three Kingdoms, arrived at Stirling.

Within the different sides there was mixed loyalties, and to further complicate matters, loyalties switched from time to time. At the end of 1647 King Charles entered into secret communication with Scottish leaders, whereby he agreed to make concessions on the religious settlement of Scotland in return for military aid. A deal was negotiated to form a new alliance, known as the Engagement, and those who supported and fought for this alliance were known as the Engagers. It did, however, split the Covenanters, as not all supported the agreement. Some of their leaders, such as the Marquis of Argyll, feared that showing loyalty to King Charles would lead to a further war with England, whereas the idea of the Engagement was gathering significant support, led by the Duke of Hamilton and Earl of Lauderdale.

A Scottish Engager army was sent to England and, after some initial successes, they met the New Model Army, under the command of Oliver Cromwell, outside Preston. Despite being smaller in numbers, the effectiveness of the New Model Army resulted in a decisive win for the Parliamentarians, with the Royalist Engagers suffering large losses.

In Scotland, Archibald Campbell, the Marquess of Argyll, a loyal Covenanter who opposed the Engagement, marched a relatively small army into Stirling where he took the town largely unopposed on 12 September 1648. The castle, however, remained under the control of those who supported the Engagement.

Upon learning that Campbell was in Stirling, Sir George Munro, an Engager general, decided to launch a surprise attack to attempt to defeat Campbell and capture his army commanders. The attack was successful; it is said that some of Campbell's forces did not even know Munro had entered the town until he himself broke into the building in which they were staying. Though Campbell's men tried to gather together and fight back, it was a short-lived effort. To add to the disorder, Archibald Campbell had already fled the town. George Munro's forces had in fact been spotted as they approached, yet when Campbell was notified he fled across Stirling Bridge to the north, under fire from the castle, rather than gather his army.

The battle was swift and decisive. Around 200 of Campbell's men, including several of his commanders, were killed in the battle, with more drowning trying to escape across the River Forth. A further 400 were taken prisoner. It was a significant

The north entrance to Kings Park. (Courtesy of Alec MacKinnon, CC BY-SA 2.0)

Mar's Wark, where the Marquess of Argyll was dining when he was notified of the approaching enemy army.

victory for the Engagers after their defeat at Preston, but one that put Stirling at risk of destruction for some time after. The Earl of Lanark, the leader of the Engagers in Scotland, had amassed an army of around 10,000 outside Stirling, whereas David Leslie, one of Archibald Campbell's generals, had gathered an army of around 11,000. It became apparent that had Munro not launched his surprise attack there would have been a full-scale battle between two massive armies at Stirling.

Despite being urged to still face each other, negotiations between both sides started, and on 27 September a treaty was agreed, known as the Treaty of Stirling, which saw both sides joining forces. This signalled a new leadership in Scotland, with power returning to the Covenanters and the demise of the Engagers' authority. On 4 October, Oliver Cromwell met with the Covenanters in Edinburgh, with discussions amicable enough for him to leave soldiers from the New Model Army to support them; however, this was all soon to change.

A forced change to the English Parliament in December 1648 resulted in agreement for King Charles to be tried for treason. When Cromwell returned to London he became a key supporter, believing that the demise of the king would end all wars in the country. The campaign was successful, King Charles was convicted and Cromwell was one of the signatories on his death warrant, with the execution taking place at the end of January 1649.

Cromwell went on to defeat any remnants of the Royalist army and England was declared to be a republic, with Cromwell appointed as the Lord Protector. The authorities in Scotland were, however, less keen on this arrangement and opted to declare Charles II as the King of Scotland. This action was seen by Cromwell as a clear act of defiance against his authority. Negotiations followed between the two sides to try to reach a resolution; however, when talks broke down in 1650, Cromwell invaded to try to take power by force. His first target was Dunbar, which would provide him with a seaport from which he could launch attacks north; however, Sir David Leslie once again rose to prominence and fought back against Cromwell's army. Cromwell in turn advanced on Edinburgh and the Port of Leith, where he was unsuccessful in breaking through the Scottish defences, resulting in him retreating to the south of Scotland again.

Sir David Leslie, enthused by his victories, pursued Cromwell and the forces met again at Dunbar on 3 September 1650. While Leslie had been successful in defending territory, an open-field battle against the highly skilled professional soldiers of the New Model Army was a very different matter. Despite having far greater numbers, Cromwell was victorious, with up to an estimated 3,000 killed in the Covenanter forces and a further 10,000 taken prisoner, compared to losses of under 100 on Cromwell's side. With Charles II at Stirling, Leslie retreated there to the safety of the castle. By holding the crossing across the River Forth, Leslie would be able to gather additional military aid from the north while preventing Cromwell from advancing further.

A memorial stone marking the Battle of Dunbar. (Courtesy of Jennifer Petrie, CC BY-SA 2.0)

In memory of the Dunbar soldiers taken prisoner at the Battle of Dunbar in 1650. (Courtesy of Jennifer Petrie, CC BY-SA 2.0)

Leslie's retreat to Stirling allowed Cromwell to seize Edinburgh. Yet, from his previous expeditions into Scotland, he knew holding Stirling would be vital for the success of his mission. The only road suitable to take a military force of the size that he was forming was through Stirling and across Stirling Bridge. He equally knew that the longer it took for him to reach the north of Scotland, the more chance there was that the clans in the Highlands would join together and form a fighting force, aided with supplies from the central belt of Scotland, that would be too large and too well equipped for even the New Model Army to defeat. Cromwell was left with a difficult decision. He held Edinburgh, but not the castle – holding onto the town, especially the Port of Leith, was vital. Stirling was equally vital, but he did not yet have enough troops to allow him to advance on Stirling while leaving sufficient numbers in Edinburgh to prevent the garrisons from the castle from retaking the town, and to advance on Stirling. He called upon the commanders to send him troops and, with reinforcements of around 2,500 men, he made his move. On 14 September 1650, leaving three regiments of troops in Edinburgh, he took his army which had landed in Fife.

When they were within 1 mile of the town, battle plans were prepared. This would include the use of ladders, which were hastily gathered to breach the walls of the town and ultimately the castle. With the attack planned for the afternoon of 17 September, Cromwell had a change of heart, which would delay the onslaught to Stirling. The remaining supplies would only be sufficient to sustain any attack for seven days, yet Cromwell knew not only how well Stirling was physically protected as a stronghold, but also of the earlier skills of Sir David Leslie at holding out in a defensive position. Even if Cromwell overcame the odds and took the town, he had already called upon all the reinforcements that were immediately available to him, and he would have insufficient men to hold both Stirling and Edinburgh against any retaliatory attacks from the Covenanter forces. Instead, he opted to return to Linlithgow, which he had taken on his approach to Stirling. His plan was to fortify the town over the winter months and create his own stronghold there to allow him to build both a sufficient army and hold sufficient supplies, later launching his attack on Stirling from there.

Cromwell spent the time wisely, expanding the territory he held in the south of Scotland where he could and continuing negotiations with any of the Covenanter commanders who would engage with him, in an attempt to secure their support without force, while all the time he was planning his next moves to take both Edinburgh Castle and Stirling. He was aware of the importance of timing his advance against the growing support for Charles II, who was officially crowned King of Scotland on 1 January 1651 at Scone, Perth, and promptly started to tour the areas north of the Forth. With King Charles officially taking control of the Covenanter forces as a Royalist army, Sir David Leslie was made second in command in recognition of his achievements. Knowing that Cromwell was building a stronghold at Linlithgow, just 26 miles away, Sir Leslie set about further improving the defences of Stirling.

On 4 February, Cromwell judged that he could wait no longer and moved towards Stirling once again; however, it was not the defences or military expertise that would save the town from attack on this occasion, but the weather. It was a particularly harsh winter, and by 7 February a large number of his troops had fallen ill and the road to Stirling was being torn up by his army travelling on it, making it very difficult for further garrisons to follow. Cromwell had no choice but to return to Linlithgow, before he returned to Edinburgh. He, too, did not come away from the failed advance unscathed, falling seriously ill from exposure to the weather conditions; it would be March before he was again well enough to focus his attention on Stirling. By this time reinforcements from London had arrived in Edinburgh, and he at last had sufficient forces. During his illness he came up with an extreme plan to take Stirling. Knowing the condition of the road and how heavily defended the town was, he formed a strategy to try to lure King Charles and Sir Leslie out into open battle.

On 27 March, four warships sailed from Leith into the Firth of Forth where they attacked the island of Inchgarvie, which was held by Royalist forces. With the island taken, they sailed further up the Forth and secured Blackness Castle. This laid the foundations for Cromwell's plans and, when he was well enough to take full command in April, he launched a naval attack on the port of Burntisland in Fife on the opposite side of the Forth from Leith, along with a land attack on Glasgow. He ensured that the land forces followed a route where they would be seen from the castle and, with word almost surely reaching Stirling of the attacks in Fife, he hoped Leslie would pursue the land forces. The initial plans failed, with both Leslie and King Charles remaining within the protection of Stirling. Cromwell once again fell ill, further delaying any more attempts.

While the first stage of Cromwell's plan had not been successful, they were laying the way for an even higher-risk strategy. He had a number of specially designed flat-bottomed boats constructed, which would be sufficient to carry a large number of troops across the Forth. The chosen crossing point was between North and South Queensferry – roughly where the railway bridge now stands. This was the narrowest part of the Firth of Forth thanks to the peninsula, which North Queensferry occupies. In addition, the attacks on the fort on the island of Inchgarvie, which lay at almost midpoint of the crossing, and Burntisland to the north, had substantially reduced any risk of counter-attack from the Scottish Royalists. On 17 July 1651, Cromwell successfully took 1,600 men across the River Forth, with a further 2,500 men making the crossing over the next two days.

It is not completely clear whether this plan was a distraction or a serious attack on the north. It worked as both. Upon learning of the landing in Fife, forces

The Forth Road and Rail Bridges. The Rail Bridge, to the right of the image, crosses at approximately the same point taken by Cromwell. (© Derek Bathgate, CC BY-SA 2.0)

were sent to repel them, including a substantial number from Stirling. Cromwell had already taken an army to the outskirts of Stirling and, upon seeing the departure of the troops towards Fife, he moved around Stirling hoping to have an opportunity to seize the town while its defences were restricted. He was blocked at Kings Park and retreated to Linlithgow.

His army was met by a hastily gathered Royalist army of around the same size at the town of Inverkeithing in Fife. In the initial stages, with the Royalists fighting from a defensive position in the hills, the battle was relatively evenly matched; however, once it reached level ground, the training and expertise of the New Model Army once again became decisive. The Royalists retreated towards Pitreavie Castle, around 2 miles away, yet were pursued all the way by Cromwell's army, suffering heavy losses, with up to 2,000 killed and 1,400 taken prisoner.

Cromwell had now secured a crossing across the Forth and, having sailed over to Fife himself, it is reported that over the following days he had amassed an army of around 14,000 men, which he marched on Perth (the main Royalist base) on 31 July. Faced with such a massive army, the town was surrendered on 2 August.

Stirling was now cut off from its supply chain in both the north and the south, and Cromwell was free to march his army north to continue his assault on Scotland. As a skilled military commander, however, he had not given up on Stirling. It had been his intention to appear to move his forces north, leaving a void in the south of Scotland. This worked, as King Charles saw the weakness to the south and decided to march his own forces from Stirling to England, where he theorised he could make substantial victories. Sir Leslie urged him against this; he knew it was a risky move as they did not know for sure what Cromwell's plans were. Yet the king could not be convinced and marched south, taking with him the bulk of the Scottish Royalist army. Leslie had no choice but to accompany the king.

Cromwell had anticipated this move all along and had one of his most trusted commanders, General Monck, positioned and ready to act, along with around 6,000 men. While Cromwell himself pursued King Charles, General Monck stormed Stirling, seizing the town and laying siege to the castle. He set up artillery batteries around the town, from which he bombarded the castle from all angles. With limited resources and without the guidance of Sir Leslie, with his military expertise, the garrisons within the castle urged the governor to surrender, which he eventually did on 14 August 1651.

A cairn in memory of the Battle of Inverkeithing. (Courtesy of Euan Nelson, CC BY-SA 2.0)

Pitreavie Castle, where the Covenanter troops withdrew to. Now converted to housing. (Courtesy of Kim Traynor, CC BY-SA 2.0)

From Stirling, General Monck continued his advance north, while Cromwell caught up with King Charles at Worcester on 3 September. It was here that his army was defeated, Sir David Leslie was taken prisoner, and King Charles managed to escape to France. Monck was successful in his campaign in Scotland and, in December 1653, Cromwell was sworn in as Lord Protector of England, Scotland and Ireland, although Monck's forces continued to face uprisings from Royalists supporters in the Highlands. Cromwell died in 1658 and was replaced by his son, Richard, who proved to have little of the military prowess of his father and resigned in 1659. After his resignation General Monck led a successful campaign to restore Charles II to the throne, although he did not return to Stirling again.

On 7 October 2019, it was reported in the national press that a number of fragments had been found in what was called a 'Royal Midden' beneath the walls of Stirling Castle. Among the finds were pieces of gunflint that were dated to be from around 1651, and possibly from the siege of Stirling Castle by General Monck.

A statue of Cromwell at Wythenshawe Park in Manchester. (Courtesy of David Dixon, CC BY-SA 2.0)

The remains of Newark Castle in Fife, home of Sir David Leslie. (Courtesy of John Allan, CC BY-SA 2.0)

5. The Jacobite Uprising

After centuries of warfare Stirling finally settled into a period of relative peace, and escaped unscathed from the first two Jacobite uprisings. The 1745 uprising, however, would bring the Jacobite forces to the town.

The Jacobite cause was to restore the Stuart dynasty after James II was exiled, with religious reasons once again being the cause. The 1745 uprising sought to have his grandson, Prince Charles Edward Stuart, better known as Bonnie Prince Charlie, restored as the monarch. Stirling, at that time, was still viewed as the gateway between north and south of Scotland due to the crossing, and remained an important town for any potential military movements.

The Jacobite army, led by Bonnie Prince Charlie, first passed by Stirling as he advanced south to launch a number of attacks in England. Although Stirling, as has already been demonstrated, was key in almost every military intervention in Scotland, the risk of losing large numbers of their forces on an attack on Stirling when their aim was to make advances into England was considered not worth taking. The castle governor had already shown his opposition to the Jacobites by having the south arch of Stirling Bridge destroyed in an attempt to stop their march south. Yet no doubt Prince Charlie was frustrated at being so close to the stronghold that was out of his grasp while he continued to England, and so left commanders in Perth to try to gather an additional army to join him on his return.

When he did return to Scotland, in a far more civilised manner than the town had seen in the past, Prince Charles wrote to the town leaders in advance to ask for their surrender, and in return he was granted unopposed access. The garrisons within the castle, however, refused to surrender and, perhaps optimistically, Prince Charles decided to make an attempt to take it by force and he laid siege to the castle.

On 17 January 1746, Lieutenant General Henry Hawley of the British army attempted to break the siege, but was intercepted and defeated at Falkirk. By this time, heavy guns had already started to arrive at Stirling. Meanwhile, relationships were becoming strained between the Scottish Jacobite commanders and Prince Charles, many saw the attempt to take Stirling Castle as pointless as they did not have any siege equipment, and the unrest was further escalated by disagreements on what to do after the defeat of General Hawley, which was seen as an indecisive win due to many of his troops being allowed to

The view of Stirling Castle from Lady's Rock, showing how it gave a vantage point being above the castle's defensive walls.

retreat to Edinburgh. It was suggested that the artillery guns should be placed at a high point close to the Old Town Cemetery. With the castle being on a rocky outcrop, the heightened position of the cannons would give a more direct firing line to the castle fortifications. Prince Charles, however, decided to site them at Gowan Hill where they would be better protected. To get the guns to this point required them to be hoisted up an almost-vertical cliff face and over a defensive wall – a process that was both slow and not without its casualties. Some reports suggest that at least one gun was mounted at Ladies Rock in the Old Cemetery. When the guns at Gown Hill were fired, they initially overshot the castle and hit the building known as Mar's Wark on the opposite side. The response from the castle garrison was swift and the Jacobites gun placements were quickly destroyed by artillery fire from the castle.

The siege on Stirling Castle was essentially over and, with many of the Highland soldiers on the Jacobite side returning north due to a long-standing tradition among the Highlanders not to launch military campaigns during the winter months, Charles' options were limited. On 1 February, his gunpowder store at

Gowan Hill, the site chosen for the Jacobite heavy guns to be positioned.

Cannons sitting on Gowan Hill. These are not the Jacobite guns, which were destroyed.

The tower of St Ninian's Church – all that remained after the explosion at the Jacobite gunpowder store. (© John Lord, CC BY-SA 2.0)

Mar's Wark, which was struck in the initial Jacobite artillery fire. (Courtesy of Lairich Rig, CC BY-SA 2.0)

Bannockburn House, where it is said Bonnie Prince Charlie stayed during his time in Stirling.

St Ninians Church exploded, destroying all but the tower of the building. There are various thoughts on this, with some feeling it was accidental while others argue it was a deliberate act. Regardless, it was the final straw for Prince Charles, who abandoned his attempts to take Stirling and returned north where he was ultimately defeated at the Battle of Culloden.

General view of Culloden Battlefield, where Bonnie Prince Charlie's forces were defeated by the British army.

6. Stirling in More Recent Times

The Jacobite uprising of 1745 was the last time Stirling Castle was laid to siege, and more peaceful times followed. Stirling grew as a market town, with cattle drovers using the bridge to take their herds south and a steamboat link being established between the town and Leith, taking goods to the larger ports for export before the railways arrived. The blockades of the Forth during the world wars would eventually, however, lead to the end of Stirling as a port town.

The importance of the town's military past was never far away from the memories of the people, and plans were first put together for a national monument commemorating Sir William Wallace in 1818. The suggested location of Glasgow did not sit well with the country's capital city, Edinburgh, and so a compromise was looked for. It was finally decided to site the monument at Abbey Craig, which in hindsight was the most fitting location as it was where Wallace's army waited and overlooked the battleground. Standing 67 meters high, the construction was no easy task, with work starting in 1861 and not completed until 1869. The monument still dominates the skyline as you approach Stirling for miles around, leaving you in no doubt of the historic importance of the town.

During the First World War, Stirling Castle became an important recruitment centre for young soldiers. It provided a facility where the recruits could stay for a few days, giving them an opportunity (albeit a brief one) to acclimatise to military life, be checked to be medically fit and be provided with the necessary equipment. Their stay at the castle also allowed them to carry out drill practice and to learn to dig and work in trenches, which was carried out at Kings Park. One of the most poignant memories those who recalled this time had was the sound of the pipers echoing around the town: young soldiers were piped out of the castle on their way to war and, for many, it was the last time they would see their native country.

Stirling did not come out unscathed from the Second World War. In 1940, the German Luftwaffe launched the only bomb strike on the town. Fortunately, the residential areas were not hit, though Forthbank Park, a sporting venue and home to King's Park Football Club, was. The sports ground and stadium were extensively damaged, resulting in the demolition of the building and the dissolution of the football club.

Across Stirling there are many more buildings that serve as reminders of the area's military past, some of which we will look at over the following pages.

It is not only monuments that commemorate the military heritage of Stirling. An annual military show known as Armed Forces Day is held at King's Park. The show provides a full programme of displays, including military bands, personnel and vehicles, a parade through the town and parachute displays. And while there are markers of Stirling's military past all around the town, the presence of the Stormtroopers of the UK garrison at the 2019 Armed Forces Day is perhaps a glimpse of the military future!

The Old Town Jail. Built in 1847 to replace the overcrowded tollbooth jail, Stirling Old Town Jail became a military prison and remained in use until 1935.

The Forthside Barracks, commonly known as the French Barracks. The Forthside estate was sold to the British army in 1864 and the buildings were used by the Royal Army Ordnance Corp. The French Barracks provided mainly storage. Now disused, the buildings are slowly being brought back into use. (Courtesy of Thomas Nugent, CC BY-SA 2.0)

The National William Wallace Monument. (Courtesy of Mike Pennington, CC BY-SA 2.0)

The Star Pyramid, commissioned by William Drummond in 1863, is dedicated to all those who suffered martyrdom in the Reformation.

This photo illustrates just how much the Wallace Monument dominates the skyline.

Above and next page: Detail on the Wallace Monument. (Courtesy of Aaron Bradley, CC
BY-SA 2.0)

This statue of King Robert the Bruce stands outside Stirling Castle, looking towards the battlefield at Bannockburn. (Courtesy of David Dixon, CC BY-SA 2.0)

These two field cannons sit close to the centre of Stirling. Made during the Napoleonic Wars, by the start of the twentieth century they were deemed surplus to requirements at the castle. A total of twelve were offered to the town of Stirling by the War Office. Assuming they were a gift and would enhance the public areas, the town council accepted, but upon discovering they were expected to pay towards the costs, they took just four. The remaining two sit on Gowan Hill.

Thoughts always turn to the Wright brothers when discussing pioneers of flight; however, Stirling had their own. Born in London in the late nineteenth century, Frank and Harold Barnwell moved to Stirlingshire while their father was the managing director of the Fairfield shipyard in Govan. They built their first glider in their garden at home before setting up the Grampian Engineering and Motor Company at Causeway, Stirling, finishing their first aircraft there in 1908. Their first successful flight across the field at Causeway, Scotland's first powered flight, was on 8 July 1909. Sadly, Harold was killed in a crash in 1917. Frank went on to design the Bristol F2 Fighter during the First World War and the Bristol Blenheim, which was used during the Second Word War, before he was killed in a crash in his own plane in 1938. A memorial to the brothers sits near to the site of their workshop and the fields where they made their first flight. (Courtesy of Euan Nelson, CC BY-SA 2.0)

The Boer War memorial, dedicated to the men of the Argyll and Sutherland Highlanders who fell during the Boer War (1899–1902) in South Africa, stands outside the castle walls depicting a soldier ready for battle and looking over the town. (Courtesy of Robert Murray, CC BY-SA 2.0)

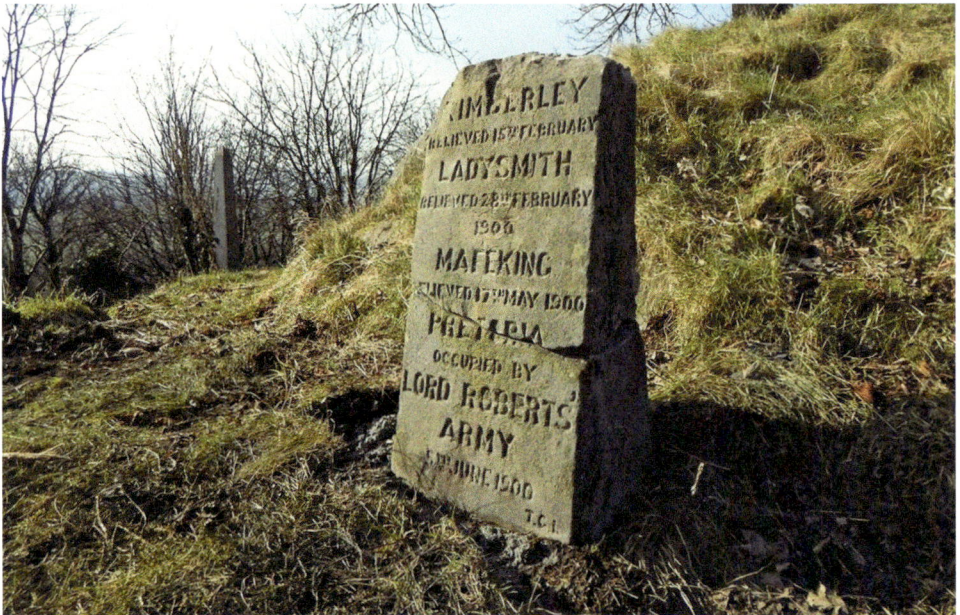

A second, far less obvious memorial to the Boer War lies at Ladies Rock in the Old Cemetery. (Courtesy of Lairich Rig, CC BY-SA 2.0)

In the car park of the Castle Esplanade there is a memorial dedicated to the men of the 75th Stirlingshire Regiment who died at Seringapatam, Delhi, during the Indian Mutiny (1857–58) and in the relief of Lucknow. Unfortunately, the memorial blew down during severe winds in the winter of 2017 and was badly damaged. It is hoped that it will be restored and returned to the location. (Courtesy of Darrin Antrobus, CC BY-SA 2.0)

Stirling's war memorial on Corn Exchange Road, built in 1922. It was dedicated to those who lost their life in the First World War and was later dedicated to those who fell in the Second World War. (Courtesy of Thomas Nugent, CC BY-SA 2.0)

Bibliography

Anon, *A General History of Stirling* (C. Randall: 1794)

Anon, *A New Description of the Town and Castle of Stirling* (Ebener Johnstone: 1835)

Chambers, Robert, *Domestic Annals of Scotland* (W&R Chambers: Edinburgh, 1859)

Lawrie, John, *The History of Wars in Scotland* (W. Darling: Edinburgh, 1783)

MacLagan, Christian, *The Hill Forts, Stone Circles, and Other Structural Remains of Ancient Scotland* (Edmonston and Douglas: Edinburgh, 1875)

Rogers, Revd Charles, *Stirling the Battleground of Civil and Religious liberties* (James Nisbet & Co.: 1857)

Sibbald, Sir Robert, *The History of the Sheriffdoms of Linlithgow and Stirling* (Andrew Stmson: 1710)

Thomson, James K., *A Bronze Age Cairn at Coneypark, Stirling* (Council for British Archaeology, N.K.)

About the Author

Gregor was born and raised in the town of St Andrews in Fife. Having been surrounded with history from a young age, his desire to learn about the past was spiked through his grandfather, a master of gold leaf work whose expertise saw him working on some of the most prestigious buildings in the country, including Falkland Palace. After talking to other staff in these monuments, he would come back and recall the stories to Gregor – normally with a ghost tale thrown in for good measure.

Growing up, Gregor would read as many books as he could get his hands on about ghost lore and, going into adulthood, his interest continued and he would visit many of the historic locations he had read about. After taking up paranormal investigation as a hobby, Gregor started to become frustrated at the lack of information available behind the reputed haunting. He has always felt it is easy to tell a ghost story, but it is not so easy to go back into the history to uncover exactly what happened, when and who were the people involved that might lead to an alleged haunting. He made it a personal goal to research tales by searching the historical records to try to find the earliest possible accounts of both what had happened, and the first telling of the ghost story, before it was adjusted as it was handed down from generation to generation. This proved to be an interesting area to research and Gregor found himself with a lot of material and new theories about what causes a site to be allegedly haunted. After having several successful books published about the paranormal, Gregor found himself uncovering numerous forgotten or hidden tales from history. These were not ghost related but were stories too good to remain lost in the archives, and he looked to bring the stories for specific towns together to tell their lesser-known history, including often the darker side.

Gregor's first book in this area was *Secret St Andrews*, telling the long and often brutal history from his own neighbourhood, and he has since written *Secret Inverness*, *Secret Dunfermline*, *Secret Stirling* and *Secret Dundee*, and a natural progression was to focus solely on the military heritage of Scottish towns and cities, with his first book in this series being *Edinburgh's Military Heritage*.

STIRLING'S
MILITARY HERITAGE

Gregor Stewart

AMBERLEY

First published 2020

Amberley Publishing
The Hill, Stroud
Gloucestershire, GL5 4EP

www.amberley-books.com

Copyright © Gregor Stewart, 2020

Logo source material courtesy of Gerry van Tonder

The right of Gregor Stewart to be identified as the
Author of this work has been asserted in accordance
with the Copyrights, Designs and Patents Act 1988.

ISBN 978 1 4456 8890 9 (print)
ISBN 978 1 4456 8891 6 (ebook)

British Library Cataloguing in Publication Data.
A catalogue record for this book is available from the
British Library.

Origination by Amberley Publishing.
Printed in Great Britain.